Honoring Genius

Books by Haki R. Madhubuti

Non-Fiction
Freedom to Self-Destruct: Easier to Believe than Think-New and Selected Essays
YellowBlack: The First Twenty-One Years of a Poet's Life, A Memoir
Tough Notes: A Healing Call for Creating Exceptional Black Men
Claiming Earth: Race Rage Rape, Redemption: Blacks Seeking a Culture of Enlightened Empowerment
Dynamite Voices: Black Poets of the 1960s
Black Men: Obsolete, Single, Dangerous? The Afrikan American Family in Transition
From Plan to Planet: Life Studies; The Need for Afrikan Minds and Institutions
Enemies: The Clash of Races
A Capsule Course in Black Poetry (co-author)
African Centered Education (co-author)
Kwanzaa: A Progressive and Uplifting African American Holiday

Poetry
Liberation Narratives: New and Collected Poems 1966-2009
Run Toward Fear: New Poems and A Poet's Handbook
Heartlove: Wedding and Love Poems
GroundWork: New and Selected Poems of Don L. Lee / Haki R. Madhubuti from 1966-1996
Killing Memory, Seeking Ancestors
Earthquakes and Sunrise Missions
Book of Life
Directionscore: New and Selected Poems
We Walk the Way of the New World
Don't Cry, Scream
Black Pride
Think Black

Anthologies
By Any Means Necessary: Malcolm X-Real, Not Reinvented (co-editor)
Releasing the Spirit: A Collection of Literary Works from Gallery 37 (co-editor)
Describe the Moment: A Collection of Literary Works from Gallery 37 (co-editor)
Million Man March / Day of Absence: A Commemorative Anthology (co-editor)
Confusion by Any Other Name: Essays Exploring the Negative Impact of
The Black Man's Guide to Understanding the Black Woman (editor)
Why L.A. Happened: Implications of the '92 Los Angeles Rebellion (editor)
Say that the River Turns: The Impact of Gwendolyn Brooks (editor)
To Gwen, With Love (co-editor)

Recordings: Poetry and Music
Rise Vision Comin (with Nation: Afrikan Liberation Arts Ensemble)
Medasi (with Nation: Afrikan Liberation Arts Ensemble)
Rappin' and Readin'

Honoring Genius

Gwendolyn Brooks:

The Narrative of Craft, Art, Kindness and Justice

Poems

Haki R. Madhubuti

THIRD WORLD PRESS

Progressive Black Publishing Since 1967

CHICAGO

Third World Press
Publishers since 1967
Chicago

First Edition
Printed in the United States of America
The production and printing of this book has been generously supported by the Lomax Companies of Philadelphia

Photos courtesy of Lynda Koolish, Esco Photos, G. Marshall Wilson, Eugene B. Redmond and Third Word Press collection.

Library of Congress Control Number: 2011940515
ISBN 10: 0-88378-325-8
ISBN 13: 978-0-88378-325-2

16 15 14 13 12 11   6 5 4 3 2 1

Dedication

Carol D. Lee (Safisha Madhubuti)

bell hooks

Derrick Bell

William Cox

Lerone Bennett Jr.

Susan L. Taylor and Khephra Burns

Beverly and Walter Lomax

William Ayers and Bernardine Dohrn

Walter Mosley

Nora Brooks Blakely

Wesley Snipes

Michael Moore

Ruby Dee

Harry Belafonte

Rev. Otis Moss Jr.

Lisa Lee

Robert Bly

and

Sterling D. Plumpp, a poet of uncompromising
beauty and power

to

all innovators and creative people

forever fighting for that which is

right, just, good and correct

and

for the students, faculty

and staff of

DePaul University, Chicago

In Memory of

Ai

Juliano Mer-Khamis

David Kato

Jim Tillman

Gil Scott-Heron

Lucille Clifton

Howard Zinn

Hannibal Afrik

Wangari Maathai

Steve Jobs

Rev. Fred Shuttlesworth

and,

as always,

Malcolm X

Contents

— I —
Honoring Genius & Craft

— II —
Art & Kindness

Contents (Continued)

— III —
Justice

— IV —
Coda

Courtesy of Lynda Koolish

— I —

Honoring Genius & Craft

Gwendolyn Brooks:

Beyond the Wordmaker–The Making of an African American Poet

"There is indeed a new black today. He is different from any the world has known. He's a tall-walker. Almost firm. By many of his own *brothers* he is not understood. And he is understood by no white. Not the wise white; not the schooled white; not the kind white. Your least pre-requisite toward an understanding of the new black is an exceptional Doctorate which can be conferred only upon those with the proper properties of bitter birth and intrinsic sorrow. I know this is infuriating, especially to those professional Negro-understanders, some of them very kind, with special portfolio, special savvy. But I cannot say anything other, because nothing other is the truth." These words, this precise utterance is Gwendolyn Brooks 1972, is Gwendolyn Brooks post-1967, a quiet force cutting through the real dirt with new and energetic words of uncompromising richness that are to many people unexpected, but welcomed by millions.

When you view Gwendolyn Brooks' work in the pre-1967 period, you see a poet, a black poet in the actual (though still actively searching for her own definitions of blackness) on the roadway to becoming a conscious African American poet or better yet a conscious African woman in America who chose poetry as her major craft. However, Gwendolyn Brooks describes her poetry prior to 1967 as "work that was conditioned to the times and the people." In other words, poetry that lept from the pages bringing forth ideas, definitions, images, reflections, forms, colors, etc., that were molded over a distance of many years–her poetry notebook started at the age of eleven–as a result of and as a reaction to the American reality. And for black people, regardless of the level of the perception of the world, the American reality has always been a battle, a real alley fight.

The early years reaped with self awareness–there is no denying this–even though at times the force of her poetic song is strained in iambic pentameter, European sonnets and English ballads. Conditioned! There is a stronger sense of self-awareness than most of her contemporaries with the possible exception of Margaret Walker. She was able to pull through the old leftism of the 1930s and '40s and concentrate on herself, her people and most of all her "writing." Conditioned! Her definitions of the world as represented in the early poetry are often limited to accommodating her work and her person to definitions that were imposed on her from the outside; and she becomes the reactor rather than the actor. She is being defined by her surroundings and by the environment that has been built around her, but the definitions and poetic direction from the Euro-American world are also much a part of her make-up. As early as 1945 in the book *A Street in Bronzeville*, we see images of womanhood, manhood, justice and race worked into memorable lines: "Abortions will not let you forget./You remember the children you got that you did not get"; and "Men hep, and cats, or corny to the jive./ Being seen Everywhere (Keeping Alive),/Rhumboogie (and the joint is jumpin', Joe),/Brass Rail, Keyhole, De Lisa, Cabin Inn./And all the other garbage cans."; and "I had to kick their law into their teeth in order to save them."; and "He was born in Alabama./He was bred in Illinois./He was nothing but a/Plain black boy."; and "Mae Belle Jackson's husband/Whipped her good last night./ Her landlady told my ma they had/A knock-down-drag-out-fight."; and "Mame was singing/At the midnight Club./And the place was red /With blues./She could shake her body/Across the floor/For what did she have/To lose?"; and "you paid for dinner. Sammy boy,/And you didn't pay with money./You paid with your hide and my heart, Sammy boy,/For your taste of

4

pink and white honey." As the quoted lines indicate, Gwendolyn Brooks is deeply involved with black life, black pain and black spirits. To seek white honey was natural; to seek anything white in those early years was only keeping within the expected, within the encouraged. However, this thing of doing the expected cannot be fully applied to Gwendolyn Brooks because the medium she worked in was that of the unexpected—"Negroes 'just don't write, especially not poetry.'" Her movement into poetry is a profound comment on her self-confidence and speaks to the poetic vision she possessed. The fact that she chose to be a poet denoted that her view of the "whirlwind" was serious and challenging—yet conditioned.

Her growth and development partially depended upon the climate of the time. Those critical years of the Thirties and Forties left deep scars of hunger and poverty, but because of a strong and closely knit family, she survived. She has always had unusual encouragement from her mother. Other major influences varied from war number two (known as World War II) to the work of Langston Hughes and Richard Wright; the Southside of Chicago where she lived and loved; Inez Cunningham Stark at the Southside Community Art Center (Gwendolyn Brooks walked off with four poetry prizes between 1943 and 1945 at Midwestern Writers' Conferences at Northwestern University), the appearance of poems in the *Chicago Defender* and *Poetry Magazine*, working with the NAACP's young people's group, her appearance in *Mademoiselle Magazine* as one of the "Ten Women of the Year" in 1945, grants from the American Academy of Arts and Letters and Guggenheim Fellowships and work in major magazines that published "American" poetry. Gwendolyn Brooks at this time, the late Forties, was concerned with the "universal fact." Her work, like that of the late Langston Hughes, has always touched at some level on the problems of blacks in America. Even allowing that, she was often singled out as the "exception" and proclaimed as an "artist"—a poet of the first rank—a poet who happens to be black; not that

5

Gwendolyn Brooks readily accepted these nebulous titles. There was little she could do about it. We must note that she received major encouragement from all quarters to accept, participate and to be grateful for whatever recognitions she received. After all, this was what everybody was working for, wasn't it? To go unnoticed is bad enough, but to go unnoticed and not eat is not a stimulus for creativity. By 1945 she had not only married, but had a son. Her family shared time that was normally used for writing and these few literary "breaks" were not only needed, but well received and actively sought after.

If *A Street in Bronzeville* paved the way, *Annie Allen* opened the door. *Annie Allen* (1949) ran away with the Pulitzer Prize–the first black person to be so "honored." After winning the Pulitzer, she now belonged to everybody. In the eyes of white poetry lovers and white book promoters, the publicity was to read "she is a poet who happens to be black"; in other words, we can't completely forget her "negroness," so let's make it secondary. Her winning the Pulitzer in 1950 is significant for a number of reasons other than her being the first person of African ancestry to do so. One unstated fact is obvious; *she was the best poet, black or white, writing in the country at the time.* Also, in winning the Pulitzer, she became internationally known and achieved a following from her own people whereas normally she would not have had access to them. She attracted those "negro" blacks who did not believe that one is legitimate unless one is first sanctioned by whites. The Pulitzer did this. It also aided her in the pursuit of other avenues of expression and gave her a foothold into earning desperately needed money by writing reviews and articles for major white publications.

In her continuing frame of reference, the confusion over social responsibility and "art for art's sake" intensified. Even though she didn't actually see herself in the context of Euro-American poetry, she was being defined in that context. She was always the American poet who happened to be Negro–the definition was always from the negative to the positive. Again, a Euro-American definition; again

6

conditioned to accept the contradictory and the dangerous. If you cannot definitively and positively define yourself in accordance with your historical and cultural traditions, how in the world can you be consciously consistent in the direction your person and your work must take in accordance with that which is ultimately best and natural for you? At this time Gwendolyn Brooks didn't think of herself as an African or as an African American. At best she was a "new negro" becoming black. Her view of history and struggle was that of the traditional American history and had not been challenged by anyone of black substance.

Annie Allen (1949), important? Yes. Read by blacks? Not many. Annie Allen, more so than A Street in Bronzeville, seems to have been written for whites. She invents the sonnet-ballad in part 3 of the poem "Appendix to the Anniad, leaves from a loose-leaf war diary." This poem is probably earth-shaking to some, but leaves me completely dry. The poem is characterized by fourteen lines with a three part alternating rhyme scheme and couplet at the last two lines. Only when she talks of "The Children of the Poor" do we begin to sense the feel of home again: "What shall I give my children? Who are poor/Who are adjudged the leastwise of the land" or "First fight. Then fiddle" or "Not that success, for him, is sure, infallible./But never has he been afraid to reach. His lesions are legion." In the poem "Truth" we sense that that is what she is about: "And if sun comes/How shall we greet him,/Shall we not dread him,/Shall we not fear him/After so lengthy a /Session with shade?...Sweet is it, sweet is it/To sleep in the coolness/Of snug unawareness./The dark hangs heavily/Over the eyes." The book has a very heavy moral tone, a pleading tone and "God's actual" in one way or another is prevalent throughout. The poems range from the ridiculous such as "Old Laughter" (written when she was nineteen years old) but included in the book:

The men and women long ago

  In Africa, in Africa,

  Knew all there was of joy to know.

  In sunny Africa

  The spices flew from tree to tree.

  The spices trifled in the air

  That carelessly

  Fondled the twisted hair.

  The men and women richly sang

  In land of gold and green and red.

  The bells of merriment richly rang.

  But richness is long dead,

  Old laughter chilled, old music done

  In bright, bewildered Africa.

  The bamboo and the cinnamon

  Are sad in Africa.

The range extends to the careful profundity of "Intermission" part three:

  Stand off, daughter of the dusk,

  And do not wince when the bronzy lads

  Hurry to cream-yellow shining.

  It is plausible. The sun is a lode.

8

True, there is silver under
The veils of the darkness.
But few care to dig in the night
For the possible treasure of stars.

But for me there is too much "Grant me that I am human, that I hurt, that I can cry." There is an over-abundance of the special appeal to the intelligence of the world-runners, even though paradoxically in part fifteen of "The Children of the Poor," she accurately notes that their special appeal to the "intelligence" had been the argument given to us ever since they raped us from Africa: "What we are to hope is the intelligence / Can sugar up our prejudice with politeness. / Politeness will take care of what needs caring."

Yet, Gwendolyn Brooks knows that politeness is not possessed by enemies of the sun, politeness does not seek to control the world; and their intelligence is as misguided as the need to manipulate every living element with which they come in contact. *Annie Allen* is an important book. Gwendolyn Brooks' ability to use their language while using their ground rules explicitly shows that she far surpassed the best European-Americans had to offer. There is no doubt here. But in doing so, she suffered by not communicating with the masses of black people.

Her work in the latter Fifties and early Sixties, like that of James Baldwin and Ralph Ellison, appealed to a wide cross-section. The mood of the land was integration. Come melt with us was in the wind. Some of us are still recovering from the burns. LeRoi Jones (now Amiri Baraka), William Melvin Kelly, John O. Killens, Conrad Kent Rivers, Mari Evans and Melvin B. Tolson's tone of persuasion was projected toward the conscience of America. They wrote as if America (or the rulers of America) had a conscience or a higher God to which it answered. They felt that America had a moral obligation to its other inhabitants, those who were not fortunate enough to be born white and Protestant. However, a close reading of Native American history in America or their own history in America would have wiped those illusions out completely. But, even then the "I'm a writer, not a black writer" madness was in the air and along with it other distortions and temptations that forever kept the writers from dealing with their African or African-American perspectives existed. They all produced important works and all, with the possible exception of Ralph Ellison, Melvin B. Tolson and Conrad Kent Rivers, had their hands on the stop sign and were getting ready to cross the continent into the Sixties. The Sixties for Gwendolyn Brooks was to be an entrance into a new life; however it didn't start with *The Bean Eaters*.

The Bean Eaters (1960) was the major appeal, the quiet confirmation of the "Negro" as an equal. She failed to question the measuring rod. Equal to what? The poems that come alive are the very personal, such as, "In Honor of David Anderson Brooks, My Father" and the title poem "The Bean Eaters." There is much black womanness in this book. Gwendolyn Brooks is careful to give black women their due, long before the women liberationists of the 1970s. Those poems that stick out are, "A Bronzeville Mother Loiters in Mississippi. Meanwhile, A Mississisppi Mother Burns Bacon," "The Last Quatrain of the Ballad of Emmett Till," "Mrs. Small," "Jessie Mitchell's Mother," "Bronzeville Woman in a Red Hat" and "Callie Ford."

The power poem is "We Real Cool," of which she says "the ending WE's in 'We Real Cool' are tiny, wispy, weakly argumentative 'Kilroy-is-here' announcements. The boys have no accented sense of themselves, yet they are aware of a semi-defined personal importance. Say the 'we' softly."

The poem "The *Chicago Defender* Sends a Man to Little Rock" is structurally tight and was socially ahead of its time, but in the final analysis again is a major appeal to morality. The last line weakens the poem with "The love-liest lynchee was our Lord." In "A Man of the Middle Class" she shows accurate vision; her criticism of the middle class may be due to the fact that she, in her personal life, refused to become a part of make-up and costumery and insists that those who take part in it are "ineffectual." She also adds, "Moreover, the 'eminent' ones, the eminent successes of the society, whose rules and styles he imitated, seem no more in possession of the answers than he; excellent examples of dimness, moral softness and confusion, they are shooting themselves and jumping out of windows." "The Ballad of Rudolph Reed" is the excursion of a black man and his family into an all-white neighborhood. By moving in, he jeopardizes the life of himself (which he loses) and that of his family. The poem shows the black man's will to "better" himself regardless of the sacrifices.

Yet, that type of sacrifice is senseless and unforgivable, and could have been avoided if blacks at that time accurately assessed their enemies. *The Bean Eaters* was the last book of this type. There would not be any completely new book of poetry published until *In the Mecca,* and *In the Mecca* "blacked" its way out of the National Book Award in 1968.

"I–who have 'gone the gamut' from and almost angry rejection of my dark skin by some of my brainwashed brothers and sisters to a surprised queenhood in the new black sun–am qualified to enter at least the kindergarten of new consciousness now. New consciousness and trudge-toward-progress." With these words Gwendolyn Brooks begins to actively seek and express a new awareness, a black consciousness. She gives greater insight into her newness when she says: "It frightens me to realize that, if I had died before the age of fifty, I would have died a 'Negro' fraction." This is the beginning of defining from one's own perspective; this perspective is what Gwendolyn Brooks would wrestle with between *The Bean Eaters* and the publication of *In the Mecca.*

Her major associations during this period of re-definition were the young writers and the "Black" writing that was part of their make-up. She, at first hand, witnessed a resurgence of what has been termed the Black Arts Movement. In every aspect of the creative act, young brothers and sisters began to call their own images, from drama to poetry, from fiction to non-fiction, from plastic arts to film, and so on. In every area of creativity black poets cleaned house and carved their own statues into what they wanted themselves to be, regardless of who was watching and with even less regard for what critics, white and black, said. She felt the deep void when Medgar Evers and Malcolm X left us.

She conducted writers' workshops with the Blackstone Rangers and other young people. She took part in neighborhood cultural events like the dedication of the Organization of Black American Culture's Wall of Respect. She lived through the rebellion in Chicago after King's death while listening with disbelief to Mayor Daley's "Shoot to Kill" orders. She lives four blocks from the Black People's Topographical Center in Chicago, the first in the nation. The murder of Mark Clark and Fred Hampton and of other blacks continued to raise questions in her mind. And the major questions were: "What part do I play?" "Where do I fit in?" "What can I do?" Her first and most important contribution was to be the re-directing of her voice to her people—first and foremost. This is what is evident in *In the Mecca, Riot and Family Pictures.* She becomes "new music screaming in the sun."

Gwendolyn Brooks' post 1967 poetry is fat-less. Her new work resembles a man getting off meat, turning to a vegetarian diet. What one immediately notices is that all the excess weight is quickly lost. Her work becomes extremely streamlined and to the point. There were still a few excesses with language in *In the Mecca,* but she begins to experiment more with free and blank verse, yet her hand was still controlled and timed. *In the Mecca* is about black life in an old Chicago landmark. This was to be her epic of black humanity. She wanted to exhibit all its murders, loves, loneliness, hates and jealousies. "Hope occurred, and charity, sainthood, glory, shame, despair, fear, altruism. Theft, material and moral." She included all the tools of her trade, blank verse, prose verse, off-rhyme, random rhyme, long-swinging free verse, the couplet, the sonnet and the ballad. She succeeds admirably with glimpses of greatness. Let's look at

"Way-out Morgan":

Way-out Morgan is collecting guns
in a tiny fourth-floor room.
He is not hungry, ever, though sinfully lean.
He flourishes, ever, on porridge or pat of bean
pudding or wiener soup—fills fearsomely
on visions of Death-to-the-Hordes-of-the-White-Men!
Death!
(This is the Maxim painted in big black
above a bed bought at a Champlain rummage sale.)
Remembering three local-and-legal beatings, he
rubs his hands in glee,
does Way-out Morgan. Remembering his Sister
mob-raped in Mississippi, Way-out Morgan
smacks sweet his lips and adds another gun
and listens to Blackness stern and blunt and beautiful,
organ-rich Blackness telling a terrible story.
Way-out Morgan
predicts the Day of Debt-pay shall begin,
the Day of Demon-diamond,
of blood in mouths and body-mouths,
of flesh-rip in the Forum of Justice at last!
Remembering mates in the Mississippi River,
mates with black bodies once majestic, Way-out
postpones a yellow woman in his bed, postpones
wetnesses and little cries and stomachings—
to consider Ruin.

And there is compassion in "a little woman lies in dust with roaches./She never went to kindergarten./She never learned that black is not beloved." In "After Mecca" her power continues with the ultimate in manhood as in "Malcolm X":

> Original
> Ragged-round.
> Rich-robust.
>
> He had the hawk-man's eyes.
> We gasped. We saw the maleness.
> The maleness raking out and making guttural the air
> and pushing us to walls.

The section on the Blackstone Rangers is outstanding. Look at "As Seen by Disciplines." "There they are./Thirty at the corner./Black, raw, ready./Sores in the city/that do not want to heal." Gwendolyn Brooks knew in her new sense of sophistication and black association that it was difficult for the sores to heal because of the lukewarm medication. In "The Leaders" she said that "their country is a nation on no map," and challenged, in "The Sermon on the Warpland," "My people, black and black, revile the River./Say that the River turns, and turn the River." In "The Second Sermon on the Warpland," she commands, "Live and go out./Define and/medicate the whirlwind." She ends the book with an image of Big Bessie:

> The time
> cracks into furious flower. Lifts its face
> all unashamed. And sways in wicked grace.
> Whose half-black hands assemble oranges

is tom-tom hearted

(goes in bearing oranges and boom).

And there are bells for orphans—

and red and shriek and sheen.

A garbageman is dignified

as any diplomat.

Big Bessie's feet hurt like nobody's business,

but she stands—bigly—under the unruly scrutiny, stands in the
    wild weed.

In the wild weed

she is a citizen,

and, in a moment of highest quality, admirable.

It is lonesome, yes. For we are the last of the loud.

Nevertheless, live.

Conduct your blooming in the noise and whip of the whirlwind.

The books *Riot* (1969) and *Family Pictures* (1970) are important for a number of
reasons other than the obvious. With the publication of *Riot,* Gwendolyn Brooks
began her association with one of the newest and most significant black publishing
companies in the world, Broadside Press, under the quiet and strong editorship
of Dudley Randall. As her poems in *Riot* and *Family Pictures* will testify,
Gwendolyn Brooks was not only asking critical questions, but seeking substantive
answers. She was very conscious of her contradictions in her own personal life,
and as best as possible–living in a contradictory situation in America-began to
systematically deal with those contradictions.

A major problem was that of Harper and Row publishers, a company she had been with for twenty-six years. Naturally, she had a certain affection and dedication to Harper and Row, even though Harper and Row seldom, and I mean that literally, pushed the work of Gwendolyn Brooks. But the decision that was to be made in regard to Harper and Row was not either/or, but: what is best for black people. And, when people begin to put their lives in a perspective of black people as a body and not as we've traditionally done–Black people as individuals–the power and influence that we seek will come about because, in the final analysis, the *only* thing that an individual can do individually is *die*. Nobody ever built anything individually.

Thus, Gwendolyn's movement to Broadside Press was in keeping with what she said in *Family Pictures:* "Blackness / is a going to essences and to unifyings." She became the doer and not just the sayer. She ended her association with Harper and Row with the publication of *The World of Gwendolyn Brooks* and sought out after new boundaries of growth, institution building and black collective association. Before she could enjoy her new comradeship with Broadside Press, other young black writers began leaving Broadside Press and going to large white publishing companies proclaiming–loud and clear–that the "Black Arts Movement" was dead and they had to look after themselves.

Here Gwendolyn Brooks was in her fifties leaving a major white publishing company (and she never accumulated any money or security; she always shared her "wealth") because of her principles and commitment and the new young whom she so admired and patterned herself after were reversing themselves going to where she had just left. This was difficult for her to understand. This would be the black integrity of Gwendolyn Brooks and would lead to her final affirmation of self.

The "death" of the Black Arts Movement as seen by some writers was, of course, only rationale for their own sick actions, was actually an excuse for the new young "stars" to move from the collective of "we, us and our" to the individuality of "my, me and I," was the excuse used so as not to be held accountable for the madness to come. Let's examine a little closer. The division that resulted is of an elementary nature and is fundamentally important to the writer if he is to remain true to himself and to his work. The cutting factor was again in the area of definition. How does a black poet (or any black person working creatively) define herself or himself and her or his work: is she/he a poet who happens to be black or is she/he a black woman or man who happens to write? The black and white "art for art's sake" enthusiasts embraced the former and the black culturally focused writers expanded on the latter adding that she/he is an African in America who expresses herself/himself, and her or his blackness with the written word and that the creativity that she/he possesses is a gift that should be shared with her or his people and developed to the highest level humanly possible. And that this "art" form in some way should be used in the liberation and education of her or his people.

Gwendolyn Brooks had worked with this same question for about ten years now and had, in her own mind, resolved it. Yet, for the young in whom she had put faith and trust, to reverse themselves made her, too, begin to re-examine her conclusions.

This is the issue. To be able to define one's self from a historically and culturally accurate base and to follow through in one's work; keeping the best interest of one's history and culture in mind is to–actually–give direction to the coming generations. If one defines oneself as a Russian poet, immediately we know that things that are Russian are important to that poet and to acknowledge this is not to *leave out the rest of the world* or to limit the poet's range and possibilities in any way.

If a poet defines oneself as Chinese we know that that designation carries with it a certain life style which will include Chinese language, dress, cultural mores, feelings, spirituality, music, foods, dance, literature, drama, politics, and so forth. If one is an Indian from India, one is first identified with a land base; is identified with a race of people; is identified with all the cultural, religious, and political advantages and disadvantages that are associated with that people whether the "poet" accepts them or not. *This must be understood.* To define oneself is to give direction and this goes without saying, that that direction could either be *positive or negative.* When one speaks of a Yasunari Kawabata or a Yukio Mishima, one first, through name association, links them with Asia. To speak of Ayi Kwei Armah, Wole Soyinka or David Diop is first to speak of Africa and then the world.

When seeking universality, one always starts with the local and brings to the universal world that which is particularly Russian, Asian, European, Indian, Spanish, African or whatever. If, in 1972, this was not clear I will concede that the "Black Arts Movement" is dead. But the overwhelming evidence shows us that by and large the majority of black "artists" at some level understood their commitment and continued educating themselves to the realities of the world more and more: if we don't look after each other, nobody else is supposed to. The "black" artist understands this.

Gwendolyn Brooks is a black poet of African ancestry living and writing in America whose work for the most part has been "conditioned" by her experiences in America. By acknowledging her Africanness, her blackness, she reverses the trend of being defined by the negative to her own definition in the positive. She, in effect, gives direction in her new definitions which, if it does nothing else, *forces* her reader to question that definition.

Why does she call herself African? To question our existence in this world critically is the beginning of understanding the world we live in. To begin to understand that we, Africans, in this country constitute the second *largest* congregation of African people outside of Africa is important. To understand that black people in this country, who number forty million upwards, will have to question why we have so little to say over domestic policy in reference to ourselves, to question *why* we have minor input in foreign policy decisions in relationship to Africa, to question why we exist as other people's door mats is important.

To question is the beginning of empowerment. Why does Gwendolyn Brooks call herself an African? Almost for the same reason that Europeans call themselves Europeans, that Chinese call themselves Chinese, that Russians call themselves Russians, that Americans call themselves Americans—people find a sense of being, a sense of worth and substance with being associated with *land*. Associations with final roots gives us not only a history (which did not start and will not end in this country), but proclaims us heirs to a future and it is best when we, while young, find ourselves talking, acting, living and reflecting in accordance with that future, which is best understood in the context of the past.

The vision of Gwendolyn Brooks can be seen in lines from "Speech to the Young":

> Say to them,
> say to the down-keepers,
> the sun-slappers,
> the self-soilers,
> the harmony-hushers,
> "Even if you are not ready for day
> it cannot always be night."
> You will be right.
> For that is the hard home-run.
>
> Live not for battles won.
> Live not for the-end-of-the-song.
> Live in the along.

The direction Gwendolyn Brooks gives to "Young Africans" is calm, well thought out and serious:

If there are flowers, flowers
must come out to the road. Rowdy!—
knowing where wheels and people are,
knowing where whips and screams are,
knowing where deaths are, where the kind kills are.

Chester Himes said that "one of the sad things in America is that they try to control Black people with creativity." And, to control your own creativity is the pre-requisite to any kind of freedom or liberation, because if you tell the truth, you don't worry about offending. You just go ahead and cut the ugly away, while building for tomorrow.

We can see in the work of Gwendolyn Brooks post-1969 positive movement from that of the sayer to the doer, where she recognizes that *writing is not enough* for a people in a life and death struggle. For so few black writers to reflect the aspirations and needs of so many (there are about three hundred black writers who are published in America with any kind of regularity) is a responsibility that should not be taken lightly. Every word has to be considered and worked with so as to use it to its fullest potential. We know that her association with young poets and writers had a great effect upon her present and future work.

Her trip to East Africa in 1971 helped to crystallize and finalize her current African association. To understand that Jews' association with Israel is not only cultural, historical and financial, but it is necessary for their own survival is to begin to deal with the real world. To understand why the Irish in Chicago sent hundreds of thousands of dollars to Northern Ireland in the 1970s is to associate people with *land* and survival. Gwendolyn Brooks by her dealing with the young poets, Broadside Press and other institutions is only "in keeping" with what other, "European" artists have always done to aid their own. By institutionalizing her thoughts and actions, she is thinking and acting in accordance with a future which will be built by nobody but the people themselves. As in her poem, "Another Preachment to Blacks," her advice is not confused, clouded, or overly simple, but it is the message of tomorrow:

> Your singing,
> your pulse, your ultimate booming in
> the not-so-narrow temples of your Power—
> call all that, that is your Poem, AFRIKA.
> Although you know
> so little of that long leaplanguid land,
> our tiny union
> is the dwarfmagnificent.
> Is the busysimple thing.

Characteristically she has said that

> My aim, in my next future, is to write poems that will somehow successfully "call" (see Amiri Baraka's "SOS") all black people: black people in taverns, black people in alleys, black people in gutters, schools, offices, factories, prisons, the consulate; I wish to reach black people in pulpits, black people in mines, on farms, on thrones; *Not* always to "teach"—I shall wish often to entertain, to illumine. My newish voice will not be an imitation of the contemporary young black voice,

which I so admire, but an extending adaptation of today's Gwendolyn Brooks' voice.

Gwendolyn Brooks was the example for us all, a consistent monument in the real, closed eyed to the beauty and strength she radiated. Above all, she was the continuing storm that walks with the English language as lions walk with Africa. Her pressure is above boiling, cooking new food for our children to grow on.

On Her Own Terms

I first met Gwendolyn Brooks as Don L. Lee in the summer of 1967 at the First Presbyterian Church of Chicago, located in Woodlawn. She was volunteering in a program organized by the great entertainer Oscar Brown Jr. as he worked to put together his musical *Opportunity, Please Knock*. Ms. Brooks, with the youth organizer and poet Walter Bradford, was teaching young members of the Blackstone Rangers creative writing. As I and a few writers of the Organization of Black American Culture (OBAC) writers' workshop walked in that summer Saturday morning, I wondered who on a nice day would be sitting in a church hall learning how to write poetry. To my surprise, there were about 14 young sisters and brothers, all sitting quietly and attentively listening to the small fingered, tough-eyed and vigorous-voiced poet explaining the intricacies of putting words to paper in poetic form. This is the dominant image that has stayed with me throughout our 33 years of a loving familyhood. She was a wise, warm, strong-willed, philanthropic, intellectual, heart-giving, patient, forthcoming, mother-kind, searching teacher and poet extraordinaire. An ocean closed in on us Sunday, December 3, 2000, at exactly 2:30 P.M. Chicago time. Gwendolyn Brooks, who could not swim but loved the water, made her transition holding the hands of her daughter, Nora, and myself at her home overlooking Lake Michigan. For most writers and readers who turned to her work, she was the melody in our music. Ms. Brooks was a poet who embraced language as if she owned it. In her small and delicate hands, she expanded language to include the Black side of life. When she published her first book, *A Street in Bronzeville* (1945), Africans born in America ceased being an afterthought or a question mark in the poetry of America.

Ms. Brooks has always put large demands on herself and us, as in "The Sermon On the Warpland:"

My people, black and black, revile the River.
Say that the River turns, and turn the River.

These are magical lines, somewhat like marching orders. Gwendolyn Brooks has been a formidable literary example for nearly three generations. Her impact is unquestionably enormous. Few other African American writers since Langston Hughes have influenced such a large and diverse readership. On June 7, 2000, Ms. Brooks turned 83 and like the River, she, in her quiet manner, looked back over a lifetime of working with language and saw her many turnings. Her motion has indeed been riverlike, a force of nature that is both unpredictable and dependable, robust and life-giving. Her place in world literature is secure and notable. However, her greatest impact has been as a key player in the literature of America and African American people. Sixty years of active writing, publishing and doing the good work of serious poetry is, indeed, a life to celebrate.

In 1989, I founded the Gwendolyn Brooks Center for Black Literature and Creative Writing at Chicago State University. A year later, a reluctant Gwendolyn Brooks joined our faculty as Distinguished Professor of English. She was already an elder and resisted but because of my persuasive powers on behalf of students and CSU's predominantly Black majority female student body, she reversed herself in terms of her own retirement. She taught a course a semester and was available for poetry readings, and would actively council with students. For over twenty years, the CSU Brooks Center hosted an annual writers' conference that attracted most if not all of the significant, midlevel, and emerging black writers and others during that period. Until 1999, Gwendolyn Brooks participated in every conference, forever encouraging us and wishing joy and good writing on all those who attended. Because of her enormous poetic and intellectual influence on others, and me, shortly after her death, we initiated one of the first Master of Fine Arts Programs in Creative Writing at a predominately Black university. We had already founded the International Literary Hall of Fame for Writers of African Descent while she was still active at the university. Over 300 hundred writers, including Gwendolyn Brooks, have been inducted.

She was a slow and careful writer. In the totality of her work there is little that will not stand the test of close, critical examination. Gwendolyn Brooks authored over 20 books of poetry, fiction, children's books, autobiographies and nonfiction. Most notable, other than those mentioned, are *Maud Martha* (1953), *The Bean Eaters* (1960), *Selected Poems* (1963), *In the Mecca* (1968), *Riot* (1969), *The Tiger Who Wore White Gloves* (1970), *Aloneness* (1971), *The World of Gwendolyn Brooks* (1971), *Report From Part One* (1972), *Blacks* (1987), *Report From Part Two* (1996) and *In Montgomery* (2001). Ms. Brooks' strength is in both form and ideas. She is a cultural writer who makes the reader work. The experience and knowledge that she transmits is as full and as rich as the artistic brilliance of Duke Ellington, John Coltrane, Charles White, Romare Bearden, Gordon Parks, Elizabeth Catlett and Katherine Dunham. Ms. Brooks' publications–her poetry, fiction, nonfiction, autobiographies and children's books–mean a great deal to writers. She is the standard which most of us use to measure our development. She is the writer whom other writers buy to send to writers. She was the writer who many of us used in writers' workshops and literature courses. She had the stature of a Queen Mother, but was always accessible and giving. Ms. Brooks was a woman who could not live without her art, but who had never put her art above or before the people she wrote about. And because of her art, she had gained unlimited acceptance among a great many of the world's people. And yes, even as the world accepted and opened its doors to this significant poet, she never forgot her people, who are centuries displaced in this land of denial and disbelief, this land of enslavement and sugar diets, of bacon breakfasts, short suns and long moons.

Ms. Brooks, until her last days, always sought memory and hidden ideas, while writing the portrait of a battered and sturdy people. She says it best in "Primer For Blacks":

Blackness
is a title,
is a preoccupation,
is a commitment Blacks
are to comprehend—
and in which you are
to perceive your Glory.

. . . .

The huge, the pungent object of our prime out-ride
is to Comprehend,
to salute and to Love the fact that we are Black,
which *is* our "ultimate Reality"
which is the lone ground
from which our meaningful metamorphosis,
from which our prosperous staccato,
group or individual, can rise.

Self-shriveled Blacks.
Begin with gaunt and marvelous concession:
YOU are our costume and our fundamental bone.

Gwendolyn Brooks was the period in our sentences and the question mark in the eyes of outsiders. She allowed only a very few people to actually touch her bones. She wrote the soul of her people. Gwendolyn Brooks' legacy will be that of poet, teacher, advocate of children and "little people" and a person who lived a life promoting kindness and poetry. She influenced over three generations of poets and writers all over this vast nation. Her eulogy has been read and the tributes have been given; none of us *have to* search for words, bite our tongues or lie. We can all tell the truth, she loved us and we loved her. With the wind in her hand, as in trumpeter blowing, as in poet singing, as in sister of the people and of the language, she can now rest and smile at her work. Her harvest is coming in bountifully. These poems represent over thirty-three years of familyhood and more.

Poetry

Poetry will not stop or delay wars, will not erase rape
  from the landscape,
will not cease murder or eliminate poverty, hunger or
excruciating fear. Poems do not command armies, run
school systems or manage money. Poetry is not
intimately involved in the education of psychologists,
physicians or smiling politicians.

in this universe
the magic   the beauty   the willful art of explaining
the world & you;
the timeless   the unread   the unstoppable fixation
with language and ideas;
the visionary   the satisfiable equalizer screaming for
the vitality of dreams   interrupting false calm
demanding fairness and a new   new world are the
poets and their poems.

Poetry is the wellspring of tradition, the bleeding
connector to yesterdays and the free passport to
  futures.
Poems bind people to language, link generations to
each other and introduce cultures to cultures.

Poetry, if given the eye and ear, can bring memories,
issue in laughter, rain in beauty and cure ignorance.
Language in the context of the working poem can
raise the mindset of entire civilizations, speak to
two-year-olds and render some of us wise.

To be touched by living poetry can only make us
    better people.
The determined force of any age is the poem, old as
ideas and as life-giving as active lovers. A part of any
answer is in the rhythm of the people; their heartbeat
comes urgently in two universal forms, music and poetry.
for the reader   for the quiet seeker
for the many willing to sacrifice one syllable
mumblings and easy conclusions
poetry
can be that gigantic river
that allows one to recognize
in the circle of fire
the center of life.

— II —

Craft
& Kindness

Gwendolyn Brooks

she doesn't wear
costume jewelry
& she knew that walt disney
was/is making a fortune off
false eyelashes and that time magazine is the
authority on the knee/grow.
her makeup is total-real.

a negro english instructor called her:
    "a fine negro poet."
a whi-te critic said:
    "she's a credit to the negro race."
somebody else called her:
    "a pure negro writer."
johnnie mae, who's a senior in high school, said:
    "she & langston are the only negro poets we've
    read in school and i understand her."
pee wee used to carry one of her poems around in his
    back pocket;
    the one about being cool. that was befo pee wee
    was cooled by a cop's warning shot.

into the sixties

a word was born . . . . BLACK

& with black came poets

& from the poet's ball points came:

black doubleblack purpleblack blueblack been black was

black daybeforeyesterday blackerthan ultrablack super

black blackblack yellowblack niggerblack blackwhi-te- man

blackthanyoueverbes $^1/_4$ black unblack coldblack clear

black my momma's blackerthanyourmomma pimpleblack fall

black so black we can't even see you black on black in

black by black technically black mantanblack winter

black coolblack 360degreesblack coalblack midnight

black black when it's convenient rustyblack moonblack

black starblack summerblack electronblack spaceman

black shoeshineblack jimshoeblack underwearblack ugly

black auntjimammablack, uncleben'srice black williebest

black blackisbeautifulblack i justdiscoveredblack negro

black unsubstanceblack.

and everywhere the

lady "negro poet"

appeared the poets were there.

they listened & questioned

& went home feeling uncomfortable/unsound & so-

       untogether

they read/re-read/wrote & rewrote

& came back the next time to tell the

lady "negro poet"

how beautiful she was/is & how she had helped them
& she came back with:

>how necessary they were and how they've helped her.

>the poets walked & as space filled the vacuum between

>them & the

lady

"negro poet"

u could hear one of the blackpoets say:

>"bro, they been callin that sister by the wrong name."

(1968)

She Was Kindness

she was always for the least of us
the slow readers,
loud voice-less,
tooth-missing smilers,
she urged the rage in those without questions
the book silence people,
the half meal a day children,
the no tie wearers,
she gave resources and gladness to the giftless
wondermakers finding their voices,
first library users and recent readers,
children speaking first words into poems,
she taught wisdom-search and unhurried language find.

name her ocean, sea, river, and brooks,
in this opening century of war & wars
her narrative remains kindness.

(2011)

An Afterword: For Gwen Brooks

(the search for the new song begins with the old)

knowing her is not knowing her.

is not

autograph lines or souvenir signatures & shared smiles,

is not

pulitzers, poet laureates or honorary degrees

you see   we ordinary people

just know

ordinary people

to read gwen is to be,

to experience her in the *real*

is the same, she is the words,   more

like a fixed part of the world   is there

quietly penetrating   slow

reminds us of a willie kgositsile love poem   or

isaac hayes singing *one woman.*

still

she suggests more;

have u ever seen her home?

it's an idea of her: a brown wooden frame

trimmed in dark gray with a new screen door.

inside: looks like the lady owes everybody on the southside

             nothing but books momma's books.

her home like her person is under-fed and small.

gwen:

pours smiles of african-rain

a pleasure well received among uncollected garbage cans

and heatless basement apartments.

her voice the needle for new-songs

plays unsolicited messages: poets, we've all seen

poets. minor poets ruined by

minor fame.

(1971)

Poet: Gwendolyn Brooks at 70

as in music,
as in griots singing,
as in language mastered, matured
beyond melodic roots.

you came from the land of ivory and vegetation,
of seasons with large women guarding secrets.
your father was a running mountain,
your mother a crop-gatherer and God-carrier,
your family, earthgrown waterfalls,
all tested, clearheaded, focused.
ready to engage.

centuries displaced in this land of denial and disbelief,
this land of slavery and sugar diets,
of bacon breakfasts, short suns and long moons,
you sought memory and hidden ideas,
while writing the portrait or a battered people.

artfully you avoided becoming a literary museum,
side-stepped retirement and canonization,
gently casting a rising shadow over a generation of
urgent-creators waiting to make fire,
make change.

with the wind in your hand,

as in trumpeter blowing,

as in poet singing,

as in sister of the people, of the language,

smile at your work.

your harvest is coming in, bountifully.

(1987)

Quality: Gwendolyn Brooks at 73

breath,
life after seven decades plus three years
is a lot of breathing. seventy three years on this
earth is a lot of taking in and giving out, is a
life of coming from somewhere and for many a bunch
of going nowhere.

how do we celebrate a poet who has created
music with words for over fifty years, who has
showered magic on her people, who has redefined
poetry into a black world exactness
thereby giving the universe an insight into
darkroads?

just say she interprets beauty and wants to
give life, say she is patient with phoniness
and doesn't mind people calling her gwen or sister.
say she sees the genius in our children, is visionary
about possibilities, sees as clearly as ray charles and
stevie wonder, hears like determined elephants looking
for food. say that her touch is fine wood, her memory

is like an african road map detailing adventure and
clarity, yet returning to chicago's south evans
to record the journey. say her voice is majestic
and magnetic as she speaks in poetry, rhythms, song
and spirited trumpets, say she is dark skinned,
melanin rich, small-boned, hurricane-willed,
with a mind like a tornado redefining the landscape.
life after seven decades plus three years
is a lot of breathing.
gwendolyn, gwen, sister g has
not disappointed our anticipations.
in the middle
of her eldership she brings us
vigorous language, memory,
illumination.

she brings breath.

(1990)

A Mother's Poem
(for G.B.)

not often do we talk.
    destruction was to be mine at 28
    a bullet in the head   or
    wrong-handed lies that would lock
    me in pale cells that are designed to
    cut breathing and will.
you gave me maturity at daybreak
slashed my heart
and slowed the sprint toward extinction,
delayed my taking on the world alone,
you made living a laborious & loving commitment.

you shared new blood,
challenged mistaken vision,
suggested frequent smiles,
while enlarging life to more than
daily confrontations and lost battles
fought by unprepared poets.

not often did we talk.
your large acts of kindness shaped memory,

your caring penetrated bone & blood
and permanently sculptured a descendant.
i speak of you in smiles
and seldom miss a moment
to thank you for
saving a son.

(1984)

Gwendolyn Brooks:
Distinctive And Proud At 77

how do we greet significant people among us,
what is the area code that glues them to us,
who lights the sun burning in their hearts,
where stands their truths in these days of MTV
　　　and ethnic cleansing,
what language is the language of Blacks?

she has a map in her. she always returns home. we are not
open prairie, we are rural concrete written out of history. she
reminds us of what we can become, not political correctness
or social commentators and not excuse makers for Big people.
always a credit-giver for ideas originated in the quiet of her
many contemplations. a big thinker is she. sleeps with paper
and dictionary by her bed, sleeps with children in her head.
her first and second drafts are pen on paper. her husband thinks
he underestimates her. she thinks we all have possibilities.
nothing is simplified or simply given. she wears her love in her
language. if you do not listen, you will miss her secrets. we do
not occupy the margins of her heart, we are the blood, soul, Black
richness, spirit and water-source pumping the music she speaks.
uncluttered by people worship, she lives always on the edge of

significant discovery. her instruction is "rise to the occasion,"

her religion is "kindness," her work is sharing and making words

matter. she gives to the people everybody takes from.

she is grounded-seeker. cultured-boned.

she is Black sunset and at 77 is no amateur.

rooted willingly and firmly in dark soil, she is last of the great oaks.

name her poet.

as it does us, her language needs to blanket the earth.

(1994)

Mothers

(for Mittie Travis (1891-1989),
Maxine Graves (1924-1959),
Inez Hall and Gwendolyn Brooks)

"Mothers are not to be confused with
     females who only birth babies"

mountains have less height
and
elephants less weight than
mothers who plan bright futures for their children
against the sewers of western life.

mothers making magical music miles from monster madness
are not news,
are not subject for doctorates.

how shall we celebrate mothers?
how shall we call them in the winter of their lives?
what melody will cure slow bones?
who will bring them worriless late-years?
who will thank them for hidden pains?

mothers are not broken-homes,

they are irreplaceable fire,

a kiss or smile at a critical juncture,

a hug or reprimand when doubts swim in.

a calm glance when the world seems impossible,

the back that america could not break.

mothers making magical music miles from monster madness

are not news,

are not subject for doctorates.

mothers instill questions and common sense,

urge mighty thoughts and lively expectations,

are impetus for discipline and intelligent work while

making childhood exciting, unforgettable and challenging.

mothers are preventative medicine

they are

women who hold their children all night to break fevers,

women who cleaned other folks' homes in order to give their

        children one,

women who listen when others laugh,

women who believe in their children's dreams,

women who lick the bruises of their children and

give up their food as they suffer hunger pains silently.

if mothers depart their precious spaces too early

values, traditions and bonding interiors are wounded,

morals confused, ethics unknown, needed examples absent

        and

crippling histories of other people's victories are passed on as
    knowledge.

mothers are not broken-homes,
they are gifts
sharing full hearts, friendships and mysteries.
as the legs of fathers are amputated
mothers double their giving
having seen the deadly future of white flowers.

mothers making magical music miles from monster madness
are not news,
are not subject for doctorates.

who will bring them juice in the sunset of their time?
who will celebrate the wisdom of their lives,
the centrality of their songs,
the quietness of their love,
the greatness of their dance?
it must be us,
able daughters, good sons
their cultural gift,
the fruits and vegetables of their medicine.

We must come like earth rich waterfalls.

(1991)

This Poet: Gwendolyn Brooks at Eighty
June 7, 1997

this poet, this genuine visionary,
this carrier of the human spirit,
this chronicler of the Blackside of life,
this kind and gentle person is the reason
we lend our voices to this day.

that other poets have championed good writing
and literature, have exposed evil
in the world, have contributed mightily of personal resources
to the young, to the would-be-writers,
to students and to the institutions of common good
is without a doubt. however,
the only poet who has made it a mission
to incorporate all of this and more into a wonderful and
dedicated lifestyle is Gwendolyn Brooks.

without press releases, P.R. people or interpreters
from the academy the great work of this quiet poet
has touched a city, this state, our nation and the world.
her poetry, her children's books,
her essays and her autobiographies have given us an insight
into the complexities of the Black human condition

that few writers can match, yet we all try
she *is* our standard.
seventy years of writing do make a difference.

we gratefully and gracefully walk in her shadow,
not because she needs or requests that we do so;
it is that her work,
her outstanding contribution to Black literary music
in this world that demands the best from the least of us.
at eighty she needs no introductions or encouraging words.
at eighty the notes she writes to herself
are more comprehensive and in larger letters.

at eighty her walk is slower and her eyesight less certain.
at eighty she loves silence, is never voiceless or alone,
at eighty, Blackness remains her star and
she alerts her readers always to the huge possibility
of knowing one's self, others,
and the mystery and joy of a full life.

she has approached 320 seasons
on her own terms.
she has taken the alphabet and structured a language.
she has walked thousands of miles carrying her own baggage.

she has done the work she aimed to do,
children call her "Mama Gwen" and memorize her lines.

that which is "incomplete" is at her home

on the dining room table, in neat piles

enclosed in all size packages,

opened and unopened,

here and only here is where she will always be behind

she is the last of the great

handwritten letter answerers and

she will not be able to keep up with this volume of

love.

(1997)

Eighty-three is a Wise Number

The weather does not age, it
changes
bringing peach and hurricanes,
water
and sun for planting, walking
and smiles
extending people to long life,
maybe.

I've grown up in your magic,
shadows and words,
I've seen you manage pens,
paper, poor eyesight and gift
giving.
I've measured the recent dip in
your walk,
noting the way the wind leans
you into its current
and I worry.

What if I'm not there to catch
your arm

to gently steer you away from a
fall, missed step
or from harm's way

but you've always been your
own clock
and as the seasons disappear
and rise
you know exactly what time it
is,
beating the beat in storms not
of your making.

for Gwendolyn Brooks at 83

(2000)

Gwendolyn Brooks Illinois State Library:
The Naming, June 6, 2003

your ancestry is book country,
able bones crossing the atlantic ocean to discover
white pages, protein and protégé in the midland.

in my first days of learning I remember eyeglasses that joined
your smile.
I recall your fingers, long, thin, delicately brown and touchable,
suited for turning book pages, appropriate for ink sculpturing
on paper.
fingers connected to memory, a people, a culture,
Chicago and this state.
using the language of 47th street, Springfield and Cambridge,
your poetry
silences us with its narrative love-songs, ripe-sources
and bone-truths.
poems that governed the weather, invented eyes the colors
of wheat, sky, coal,
cabbage, soybeans and yes, creating images out of empty
pockets and kitchenettes.
art that reversed massacred thought, healthy words renouncing
ignorance, providing a

landscape of glorious literature

emphasizing lineage, liberty and validation.

your discourse is of children, the four seasons:

poetry that deciphers myths.

your writing: the impulse to arrive at meaning, life-ringing

idioms, bright-calm

all accenting wisdom that affirmed in us the kindness

of your grand spirit,

the friendliness of ideas, melodies and soap operas,

of water, sun and clean fire. your language is of

the necessity of carrot juice, broccoli and fattening chocolate,

of solitude, good pens and fine paper,

the labor of writers, poets, musicians and under-fed artists,

of librarians, libraries, books and break-even bookstores,

the support of printers, editors and struggling book publishers,

of book festivals, newspapers, magazines and twice-a-year

quarterlies,

the requirement of contemplation, dialogue with others

and reading on trains,

of legislators thinking outside the prism of dark suits

and half-stories.

our ancestry is book country and rich earth,

galloping souls and skillful deal makers.

we are becoming the portrait of your right words.

(2003)

Her first name was Gwen:
Last note and poem

Last Note

For over six months after her death I was just about nonfunctional. Thirty-three years of a loving familyhood with Gwen and Nora have been an integral part of my life. As cultural mother, serious friend, mentor, God-mother to our daughter, extraordinary encourager and emotional/financial supporter of Third World Press, the Institute of Positive education and our schools. Meeting her in 1967 was like rain hitting new seeds of corn in an excellent harvest year. She, in her quiet but determined manner, was able to cut into my young cool and turn it warm inviting to the genuine warmth of her personhood. I began to smile.

In 1970, I had truly become a part of her family along with her husband Henry (a fine poet himself), her daughter Nora (very creative with a strong interest in children's theatre) and her son, Henry whom I did not meet until later in our relationship. Of the men and women who had a profound impact on my early development—Malcolm X, Margaret and Charlie Burroughs, Dudley Randall, Hoyt W. Fuller and Barbara Ann Sizemore—Gwendolyn Brooks' hand remained the truest with the most artful and surgical cut. She literally transformed and saved my life.

Gwendolyn Brooks was the first person, artist, poet with national presence that I met who was realistically modest without a self-congratulatory organ in her body, fully aware of her weaknesses and never took herself too seriously.

Yes, it was the poet, artist and her unique dedication to that which was good, just, correct and right that pulled me into her family. However, I stayed there for over three decades because of the defining characteristics of her wonderful life.

As Don L. Lee I had minor fame that was too consuming and I decided in conversations with her and others to change my name to Haki R. Madhubuti (which she was not in full agreement with). Yet she understood the pull that the culture had on me thus restricting me to be as authentic as she and I wanted. With the new name and off the poetic popular grind, I turned my energies toward rebuilding: local institutional structures, completing an MFA in creative writing at the university of Iowa, creation of the GB center at CSU, my family and extended family as well as heightening my teaching and working in local, international, political, cultural activities. Writing my books and publishing the creative works of others remained a passion. Third World Press had become Gwen's primary publisher. We published, in her lifetime, ten of her books and three studies of her work by renowned scholars.

Her attachment to my bones remained nourishing, a friendly daily dose of calcium that allowed the joints in my writing hand to continue on their mission. As was she, my notes to paper into poems, essays, and occasional fiction is the clear mandate that one does not have control over. She left excellent creative baggage with thousands and with me.

Her first name was Gwen

she wrote in a small 2.5 x 3 inch-lined
white paper notebook with penpencils that she
carried wrapped in rubber bands in
small handbags that accompanied her
on trains, buses and cars with public seating
that kept her close to her people,
subjects and the disconnected impoverished
who frequented salvation army & big box stores,
used furniture warehouses and yard & garage sales.

she spoke in smiles, critical hearing and patience
under the scarves that covered her graying natural
that distinguished her small brown-black face.
she took her poem-makings from her notebooks and
translated them to type on a small portable
that lived in her bedroom along with
books, ideas and clean questions that
rejuvenated the music in her lines and mind.

she gave us the over/under side of community that
all artists perfect on their own avenues.
she was our boulevard who understood
that the black, white, red and yellow narratives of the unspoken.
art was her language, poetry the confirming letters and
Gwen was her preferred brand.

Gwendolyn Brooks: No Final Words

somewhere between brilliant and genius,

in the neighborhood of great and unforgettable,

as unique wordgiver and kind heart,

she emerged as our able witness and deep participant

in a time of unwellness and deep need.

refusing to tap dance with the garbage men of rulership,

corporate acceptance or literary sainthood,

she deciphered the multiple layers of accommodation

that often trap the best of us.

she refused first class passage and caviar.

she sidestepped isolation, re-enslavement and tell-lies culture.

she remained attached to her language,

her people and all children.

she was our kindness.

there will be no final words

— III —

Justice

Master of Colors and Canvas

how did we arrive?
mothers as artists and seers
as earth toilers, sun consumers
workers at midnight and dawn
nurtured us with apples, bananas, open hearts, seeds,
cultural language, illustration and institutions.
lovingly cut the umbilical cord,
not the commitment or sacred findings.

you with the brushes, canvas, paint, tools and ideas
with African hair, mind and memory
instigated an uprising to change the conversation
quickening our run toward saneness, smiles and fear
out-pacing a leadership who moves
like roaches with alzheimers.

today, we, on jet powered roller skates
still eat your dust
still are wondrous of the measure
of your gifts.

For Dr. Margaret T. Burroughs
On the occasion of The Art Institute of Chicago,
Leadership Advisory Committee,
Legends and Legacy Award Celebration, October 22, 2010

In A Time of Devastation and Reflection

1.

and then, the earth cracked

breaking life,

legs, street corners, tomorrows

prompting whys, whats, wheres, next?

necessitating recalls of history,

psychology, stolen economies, foreign armies,

the underside of traitors

dressed in europe, the new world

and the betrayed colors of self & self.

and then, the earth separated.

an updated missed message eclipsed

man-made catastrophes by the millions.

as children consume contaminated water & dirt,

as helicopters dropped paratroopers & excuses

on a nation unprepared for the emptiness of

international promises, smiles, hedge funds

and calls for self-reliance & reparations.

2.

and yes, a u.s. vetted world responded
with care, funds and tears,
with monies, controlled and paralyzed
by suspected off-shore agencies,
charities & wolves.
unaware of local stories, poems and culture,
ignorant of failed rulerships, ruled and braided hair.

what of the children?
of the clear, clean, innocent, muted voices
in the conflicted question of resettlement, reconstruction
and land ownership all following the money
on this soil of caste, class and color
whose cries will go unnoticed by
davos, capitol hill, 10 downing street, the G-20
and the descendants of napoleon bonaparte
and his defeated armies and history.

3.

haiti has returned to its creation
bricks, rocks, sand, dirt & tree-less.
who will plan their rebirth,
lead a reverse brain drain,
issue calls for poets, architects, musicians,
earthquake engineers, doctors, teachers, writers &
caretakers of the earth?
who will accurately define haiti's enemies,
those who are black & black,
white & white, multicolored
with the starting image of new thought, work, honest visions?

after haiti's national burial,
grieving and
the healing of the least of us
who will demand comfort and renewal,
enlightened governance and beauty.

hopefully, not the same old suspects in black suits.
certainly, you can call my name.

for Edwidge Danticat, Dr. Ron Daniels
and the people of Haiti

Politicians, Preachers and
The Reinvented University or
The Return of the H.N.I.C &
The Devastation of Liberated Thought

why *click* why *click click*

why why *click* why do *click* take this picture

why do negroes *click click* still *click*

why do negroes still rule *click* incomplete

that's an incomplete inquiry

why do negroes still rule negroes?

that's the fore question that mindless people

never ask mindless people

from africa to the americas

from the caribbean to the south/west side of chicago *click click*

from willie's grocery store on life-support selling kool-aid, nothings,

penny cookies, lottery tickets and fifty-cent dill pickles *click*

why do fools fall in love with theyselves *click*

sounds like michael jackson in bollywood or wonderland *click*

cd be tiger woods tripped up by email and denial of his blackhood or

whitney houston chasing bobby brown down a tunnel of past return

on reality tv *click click click*

where is garvey? dead *click*

where is malcom? dead *click click*

where is medgar? dead   *click click click*

where is martin? dead   *click click click click*

where is ms rosa, sister ella, harriet tubman and ida b wells? dead   *click*

where is sncc, original core, sclc, dubois' naacp?

where is the change conversation

black arts movement?   *click click*

and the historical interpretations of the others?   *click*

who is minding the unmarked graves in mississippi, alabama, south carolina,

georgia

and the white house lawn?

what did they die for? so negroes cd be free, stupid

free?   *click*   free?   *click*

free to perfect the art of the back road, under-dress deals,   *click*

free to time-share in vegas, hell and the Bahamas,   *click*

free to master they golf and investment games,   *click*

free to treat they women like overused toilet tissue,

free to birth children by the thousands for others to raise,

free to send their children to be taught by people who do not like them,   *click*

free to hate themselves, anybody that looks like them and

anybody that closely questions their self hatred.

click, click,   the unanswered question is

why is it easier to believe than think? what?   *click*

why is it easier to believe than think? what about   *click click*

give you a quarter for an original idea not about

sex, money, fame, status, white power, religion, food, sex, shoes,

white women, sex clothes, cars, white men, jewelry, sex, multiple homes or

gold-laced-fingernails designed by sweat shop asians or

pig-bellied preachers in oversized ten buttoned suits   *click* how did a mindful people become mindless?

they worshipped low information television, radio & sunday morning sermons

where they were nurtured on bar-b-que donuts dipped in sugar,

salt, and loss or memory grief.

witness negro preachers walking into a room of

angry and loud black men

and quiet the room with two words, let's pray,

translation, let's betray,

playing with god like she is stolen money and fried chicken

much easier to believe than think

they

betrayed original thought & mama's wisdom   *click*

betrayed a history written in swollen feet, blood and

the broken necks and backs of black men   *click click*

betrayed the initial content of liberated minds, what you say?   *click*

betrayed choreographed freedom songs & moves with

buck dancing & minstrel grins   *click*

betrayed the questions before the answers-right on, right on   *click*

betrayed the smiles of children thinking what you think,   *click click*

betrayed centuries of struggle against head negroes in charge

talking black, acting and sleeping white

with shoe polish lips & open asses flushing decayed blood droppings,   *click click*

how did a mindful people become mindless?

they forgot original content, history & traditions

built upon the first thoughts and essential love

they lost the precious ideas of civilizations, art, science, architecture and

humanity that issued in beauty, smiles willing work,

peace be still and spiritual yeses, critical definitions of people-hood,

they lost the love of self, people and the will to nurture children
competently, completely yet simply complex
from something to something better and best.   *click click*
how did a mindful people become mindless?   *click*
they failed to exterminate the most effective weapon & invention
ever coneived for their demise and control by white supremacy:
colored nuclear bombs guaranteeing
the hostile takeover of african-black life, love, liberty & institutions
by maggot-brain midgets bearing ignorant knowledge, stupid intelligence
with mouths fashioned as shotguns
at the ready only to be used against
one's own people, blood, children and culture.
welcome into the mind's eye and the central organs of the negro volcano.
poets, scholars, hand-workers, writers & cultural warriors in mass needed
now and now.
click   click   click

For Malcolm X, Betty Shabazz and Gwendolyn Brooks
and their life's work of liberated thoughts & actions

Emergence:
Brotherman Becomes a University President

in the hearing
in this time of distilled knowledge where
european ghost have displaced a people and memory,
disrupted public gardens with bullets, lies, false gods & globalization,
rearranged cultures, families and indigenous story-telling,
dressing this and more as the truth, end poems and future,
renaming our babies, rewriting the texts, claiming impossibilities,
until.

calling the question
is there justice and rightness in our heads and hearts
where such is argued and often is fiction of the
lowest calamity occupying the compressed shelves of
supermarket bookstores beside twinkies, saturated fats
and sugared cereal boxes advertising the latest junk from china.

notes for exceptional ears,
if there is good and a desire for correctness   now
burning for wise answers within this tower of intellect,
inquiry, innocent eyes, deep research and professor's smiles.
this is his fate and last step   calling him

brother, husband, baba, typical one, fearless son
a teacher-man embodying the sacred themes & rules of basketball
who will not betray malcolm, king, medgar, baker,
ms. rosa or four Black girls kneeling in birmingham before
their god to be brutally torched, taken and touched by history.

as others went into hiding (low information hustlers)
you stood ground championing the scholar's road
you, a used book on loan to students world over,
you, a learned choir chanting the integrity be-bop
creating character and intercepting evil disguised as
market share, derivatives and celebrity-hood unable to think
beyond surface & pleasure showered in half-truths & facade.

calling is confirmed   Dr. David Hall
you are our spiritual sage, illuminator, son, brotherman, husband,
baba, fifth president of the University of the Virgin Islands,
as in black stone, urban rock, rooted African, green greens,
cleansing trees, deep well water, sun mountain rising, our rare book
deciphering languages, a master of the first way.
welcome native soul as we, on this day 3-6-2010,
place your name in this earth,
at this institute of enlightened wonderment.
let the family join this calling.

ashe   ashe   ashe

For Dr. David Hall
New President of the University of the West Indies

Keeping Papers Alive

books altered the culture of his life,

a DNA effect that transported him southwest of

wherever he was meant to be.

yes, books, journals, magazines and newspapers with

multiple titles, designations and signatures

created in the forms of handwritten prose, typed poetry,

un-deciphered african languages, scholar's codes and

playwriter's words, nuances and stage props

all spoke to him in rooms never destined to be his,

small archival spaces amended before he understood the

canons of layered languages rinsed in

garlic & hot sauce mixed with black chocolate, negro bottom ideas

located on that same southeast corner of southwest chi-town.

defending and contemplating memories of woodson, hughes,

wright, brooks, colter, perkins and burroughs—all

engraved permanently, affectionately among peers and others where

readers, scholars and community cluster—

encouraged, given pens and bottles of ink.

reminding us of earlier writers/poets who craved the feel of

black ink to paper creating and exploding ideas, images,

themes, characters and then some to

insure that our world advances its logical protocols.

you leave prodigious fingerprints.

On the Retirement of Michael Flug from The Carter G.Woodson
Regional Library of The Chicago Public Library—2010

Turning Toward Joy

it is the goodness in these anointed souls,
two middle-love wonderments supplying breath to the other
mastering art, silence, political slaps and wondrous music.
whole voices are heard in the midst of double joy.
come quiet, come smiling, come as assured lovers
in barbados summer's january for this joining.

millet, flowers, ripe fruit and tenderness surround r. & r.
in a decade of terror & danger they protect each other's heart.
they are bookends, palm trees, brooklyn stop signs & bone true.
not islands, their love is a continent of perceptive rivers feeding lakes
among clean wishes and whispers tuning our ears southward.

absolutely acknowledging sacred learning and spiritual answers,
declaring permanent inquiries of we've arrived,
you, together, taste the juice, water & bread of each other's delicate touch.
clear perfection confirms africa and the diaspora,
honors tradition, family, ancestors and future.

your melody is enlightened oxygen summoning life, promises and yes.

you share breath.

For Rashida Irene Bumbray and
Rashid Kwame Shabazz
1.15.2011

74

Denied Substantial
And
Fundamental Creation

it is now in the

who

you love that may

determine that you

die

without regard to the

human-person perfected in you as

caregiver, musician, educator, linguist, parent,

carpenter, spit and polish marine, visual artist, son, daughter,

actor, professional entertainer, m.d., student, clear-thinker,

athlete, interior designer, book editor, looking-for-work dog walker,

spiritual gift-giver seeking the beautiful side of yes

in a world of no and demonization of the "other"

by the "righteous" of all cultures who misread and

interpret the cultural, canonical, spiritual texts of the last millennium

as if they speak lovingly or accurately to the

human condition & intelligence, global warming, internet searches,

high speed rail, space stations, the imagination of artists,

the vision of architects & mathematicians,

the biology of love within & across languages, borders & hearts

escalating the genetics of internal bonding

with the same sex and melody as all species naturally do.
what god ordered the hammer repeatedly into his head
because he openly lived & loved the way
he was created to do by his/your
God?

For David Kato, the Ugandan gay activist who was
assassinated as a result of his work and life struggles
against madness in his native country

Critical Ignorance

functioning normally yet
dangerously stupid, the woman from alaska
formerly vp candidate of the grand-old-party and
half-governor of the wilderness state
fails to acknowledge that bad words do issue in negative consequences,
that blood libel is indeed written in the blood and lives
of a clearly defined people and their children
rekindling and magnifying a millennium of lies, hatred,
persecution, ostracism and death against
that people, their culture and religion
often forcing them to move, to run, to disperse
unwillingly around the earth as one, few and many
seldom to sleep peacefully   in part due
to the popularity and acceptance of deep ignorance
passing as knowledge from the likes of a person
who rides the avenues of monetary and political greed
in a four wheel drive while reading
bunches of stuff.

Art III
Sonia Sanchez: Drawing Fire

we were so young born into a storm
searchers in the spirit of all that was good, just, correct and
immediately right, surely possible accenting Black & African.
in the historical western theatre of hidden truths, gigantic lies
of past precious seconds raging in todays, months, years,
centuries always in the necessary acts of seeking that
which brings meaning, memory & answered solutions of Black & Blackness
issues in laughter, defines beauty neutralizing and encompasses ugly that
initiates work that encourages families within families   Black
always claiming art as the starting point of our unique journey
not yet finished as we put foot in front of foot   Black
circling ideas of resistance, liberation & mama's peach cobblers.
as we confront fear, anger, each other & the world as the
state houses, death squads & traders stole our youth and fathers
we were so young   dodging hurricanes
entering the sixties & seventies of the last century
as soldiers and youth committed to the groundwork beginning of the
Black Arts movement

art. artists. the image makers, storytellers who visualized the
best & worst of the human condition is what is missing all too much
in today's complicated arena of "what do you do?"

poet, "how you gonna make a living?"

by joining the word creators, the smile makers,

the happy hands, feet movers, doubt catchers

sub/surface explorers, idea incubators

the look you in the eye/say/yes people

where are today's impossible task takers,

the 24/7 bush women, men & young people living on promises,

coffee, the breath of lies, bad food, tea, each other, and the

wonderment of discovery from the Black Arts Movement of BAM to

the Hip Hop Movement of rain without sunshine, moon or the underside

of heat & mud, she recognized and called the young to conference

to listen as they rapped the underside of ugly teaching them to never forget

mamas, sisters, grandmamas revealed that

stopping the women stops the future

ha ha

stopping the women stops the future

ha ha ha

we stood on the shoulders of houston, wright, mckay, toomer,

tolson, danner, fanon, hayden, du bois robeson, locke, brown, cullen

garvey, washington, douglass, wheately, dunbar, woodson, well-barnett,

and the drowned voices of a people becoming whole.

in the mid-sixties of the last century   running

of a millennium that raped us from a continent we began to gain a voice

    running

as Malcolm (el-hajj malik el-shabazz) and many planted their seeds & initiated a

hurricane

that hit america and changed the course of the sun:

gwendolyn brooks, margaret walker, dudley randall, mair evans, sara webster fabio, amiri & amini baraka, broadside press. negro digest/black world, jayne cortez, motown,

don l. lee, sweet honey in the rock, larry neal, civil rights black power movements, journal of black poetry, askia toure, soul book, liberator, marvin x, eugene redmond, the philadelphia sound, kalamu ya salaam, sekou toure, third world press, nikki giovanni, black books bulletin, audre lorde, carolyn rodgers, obac, sterling plumpp, hoyt. w. fuller, john oliver killens, nation of islam, james   baldwin, ossie davis, ruby dee, sun ra, harry belafonte, coltane nina simone, ted joans, max roache, abby lincoln, johari amini, joe goncalves & martin luther king jr. sonia sanchez, sister sonia on the road always crossing borders and cultures as the blue black narrator haunted by injustice   running chanting her syllables exploring the limits of language of what is not said, said and undersaid taking the margins of life away from fear filled backrooms and lynching trees always the outsider creating loud peripheries, a first responder, as in how do we recapture hundreds of years of who we once were, how to jumpstart the minds, bodies, souls of the internet, facebook & twitter generation as to make the world right for morani and mungu and for all the children born with "you can't" in their eyes believing good health and wealth is for the other.

avoiding pigfeet, chitlins, sucking on bones and the lies of the cow's milk enthusiasts, if it has a face she will not eat it if it runs from her it will not be cooked, if she has to chase it it will not be caught or consumed, her rice is brown, her vegetables rooted green and green, her fruit consumed at the peak of ripeness, her water double filtered with a touch of lemon,

her juices fresh and slowly eaten like vitamins to organs

her shadow speaks emancipation, clarity and resistance

her voice is south african click songs

in her solitude her utterances are never anonymous

we both still believe in handwriting, note taking &

book reading page by paper page.

sonia is 100 pounds of wet raw energy

body language in words   huh

pulled from the underside of now   huh huh

spitting razor blades lyrics against euro-whites edges bent

on silencing the heroic and sheroic voices who dared question white lightening

supremacy, and our self-hatred boils in rat's blood disguised as johnny walker

red and kool-aid.

it is the artist of all cultures, in all of their many configurations who

catch breath, running, missed meals, baths & teeth brushing   running

who bent metal, blended colors, escalated love of self and others,

running lived shared lives, blows horns, beat drums   running

encouraged dancing feet and core running withstood criticism, internalized

water as in

river, sea, and ocean running often land locked, between gifted and genius

always running

against doubt, ignorance and deep poverty   running

luminous in her ability to absorb the earth's gifts and trumpet players   running

blowing unknown territories running and running whose colors

capture meaning, acute imagination and the ever present

questions of sound and sane memory running running

giving us a poet of clear guidance and off, off rhymes, haikus and

full moon of sonia

never to trip into despair or irrelevancy   running   running

go tell that.

Layla Anaya

arriving as the first madhubuti/hutchinson of the new millennium, she dropped in not as fragile or delicate breast-feeder, not as blank slate, having swam in her brilliant mother's body for three months short of a tumultuous year, with her brain wired into the trusted mind and hearts of parents ready for nothing less than breathing stone, brick, black earth washed in sea, ocean & the great lakes locked into a deeper meaning than the seven pounds, eight ounces, twenty and three-fourth inches long that she is packaged, she has parted a cloud over the earth issuing in sun, stars, and an answer to why. she emerged with a full haired head, with eyes—black and wide—that defined the urgency that she expected life. her fortune is that she has family, biological and cultural, who embraced her birth like water to an out of controlled forest fire in a time of world drought. she is our moment, our romare bearden and elizabeth catlett signature, our gwendolyn brooks and dudley randall off rhyme, our nina simone and duke ellington high swing. a gentle soul ready to rage, ready to love, who came in the morning time to awaken the day for those unable to sleep.

On the birth of Layla Anaya Madhubuti Lee
November 10, 2010

An Answer

when did they begin to sing together? what tunes grounded their hearts into one, joined their smiles, quieted each other's criticisms of the other and found them becoming the period in each other's sentences? name the hard winter, warm morning, human and animal centered river that flows between them. sounds like deep grass, uncut string beans, sautéed broccoli occasioned with the protein of underwater life-forms that nourishes them and the earth's people. she is book and history, he, music and tech. both nurtured in the Black-african-panamanian rhythms of long lineage people. quilted. they are the last of their family's 20th century deep tree births, representing moon, sun, connecting continents, memory, spirit and focused struggles. i got this. love conquers languages, finds answers in the unsaid, slow bones of this hip hop nomad who communicates in catch-lines and humor, with a body that could hide behind a toothpick. she, as teacher, cleared the right moments for analysis that trapped a part of his heart that only she knew existed; her beauty does matter, it is luminous and sticks like post-it notes with their future written in long hand. we got this. their parents as participant world-knowers, travelers that met at the a woman/a man corner of yes, to welcome their children to yesteryears, the present, tomorrow and quiet-as-it-is kept family personified and layered. always questioning and forever growing. it is tradition.

For Akili Malcolm Lee and Janeen Panisha Waller
on the occasion of their union, July 3, 2011

Cultural Daughter

the common language between us is art and family. you are exemplary in the
millet, rice and wheat fields of the talented, magnificent in music, are able to
bend a note to the curve in your ear, hear melodies and chords throughout
morning time & at midnight, are fluent in the alphabet of questioning the flats,
angles and shapes of high rhythm. you came to us over twenty years ago in
shorts-shorts, on a saturday afternoon looking for answers and work. your
willingness willed a presence that foretold the impact that night/day study,
24/7 practicing, quick called rehearsals, around the clock composing, fighting
the male ego, confronting musical patriarchs and all that goes with a company
of brilliant women declaring no to the backseat of come-get-this. it was a yes
in your flutes, a confirmation of your daughter's needs, always a challenged
motion that continually calms your many assets as you journeyed to the top
floors of your field and instrument seeking elevated articulation that quietly
separated you from the missing moments that we all need for full life and
significant architecture. i have watched you as a father, friend, mentor always
open eared to your many trails of a long and lonely step-after-step to this new
love who is measured melody and years ahead of the fears of others and your
unique voice that opens caves that had razors for locks. this god-man is an
answer and an obligation announcing in his own name a bond denoting yes.
arriving ready to define new life with this daughter/woman of uncommon
lineage, journeys, mind detection, moon chanting artist who has captured the
feet, hands, heart and head of this climatic man. she will be the comma in your

declarations; do not take her smile for granted. she has tasted bitter roots. you bring directive, summer fruits, sweet teas and solemn lyrics to her and her daughter's musical manuscripts.

For Nicole Margaret Mitchell and Calvin Bernard Gantt
on their day of union, July 10, 2011

Art

1

Art is a prodigious and primary energy force. Children's active
participation in music, dance, painting, poetry, film,
photography and the indigenous crafts of their people is what
makes them whole, significantly human, secure in their own
skin, culture and abilities. Thus, generating in them unlimited possibilities.

Art is fundamental instruction and food for a people's soul as
they translate the many languages and acts of becoming, often
telling them in no uncertain terms that all humans are
not pure or perfect. However, the children of all cultures inherit
their creators' capacity to originate from the bone of their
imaginations the closest manifestations of purity, perfection and
beauty. Art at its best encourages us to walk on water, dance
on top of trees and skip from star to star without being able to
swim, keep a beat or fly. A child's "on fire" imagination is the
one universal prerequisite for becoming an artist.

2

Magnify your children's mind with art,

jumpstart their questions with art,

introduce your children to the cultures of the world/through art,

energize their young feet, spirits and souls with art,

infuse the values important to civil culture via art,

keep them curious, political and creative with art,

speak and define the universal language of/beauty with art,

learn to appreciate peace with art,

approach the cultures of others through their art,

introduce the spiritual paths of other/people through their art.

keep young people in school, off drugs and

out of prison with art,

keep their young minds running, jumping

and excited with art.

examine the nurturing moments of love,

peace and connecting differences with art.

3

Art allows and encourages the love of self and others. The best
artists are not mass murderers, criminals or child molesters;
they are in the beauty and creation business. Art is elemental
to intelligent intelligence, working democracy, freedom, equality
and justice. Art, if used wisely and widely, early and often
is an answer and a question. It is the cultural lake that the
indigenous rivers of dance, music, local images and voices
flow. Art is the waterfall of life, reflecting the untimely and
unique soul of a people. Art is the drumbeat of good and great
hearts forever seeking peace and a grand future for all
enlightened peoples. For these are the people the world over
who lovingly proclaim, "give the artist some," kind words,
financial support, yeses from your heart, knowing intuitively
that there will be creative reciprocity in all that they give us.
Why? Because fundamentally art inspires, informs, directs,
generates hope and challenges the receiver to respond.
And finally, and this is consequential, the quality of the art
determines the quality of the responses.

libraries, librarians:
the careful equalizers

they honor the laughter of children
appreciate that it is committed, uninhibited,
innocent and essential in creating wholeness
in the welcoming eyes of our tomorrows   all
thriving on literary nourishment, love and wonderment.

they build spaces that jumpstart and augment our children's
fresh call for colors, light, green avenues, playfulness,
filtered water, large-mindedness, other children, outdoor truths,
cultural sharing, fun, adventure, answers, and clean air.

they are watermelon to this young thirst.

with the book as groundwork, stepladder, and solid stone
anchoring the center place of good thoughts and civilization,
libraries and librarians embrace the public in their name
demanding that the poor, comfortably secure, illiterate, silent questioners
big idea disciples, teachers, new technology carriers, pen & pencil users,
language deciphers, creative culture makers, the quiet and rambunctious,
sacred and secular, reserved and profane, classroom helpers & professors,
newspaper and magazine deadliners, risk takers & slow thinkers,

thesaurus & dictionary collectors, inventors, investors and beginning scholars
all apprentice in their quest for wisdom, joy, yeses and acceptance.
libraries and librarians in cities, storefronts and no fronts, on rural roads
push forward a mass-based literacy & music as much of the world discredits
truth sharing. their contemplations are local, urgent and universal in their
advocacy for knowledge as preventive medicine, defining
libraries as anti-ignorance, free, indispensable and authentic.

For Mary A. Dempsey,
Commissioner of Chicago Public Library
and for Librarians worldwide

— IV —

Coda

Young Heroes–II
To Don at Salaam

I like to see you lean back in your chair
so far you have to fall but do not—
your arms back, your fine hands
in your print pockets.

Beautiful. Impudent.
Ready for life.
A tied storm.

I like to see you wearing your boy smile
whose tribute is for two of us or three.

Sometimes in life
things seem to be moving
and they are not
and they are not
there.
You are there.

Your voice is the listened-for music.
Your act is the consolation.

I like to see you living in the world.

Gwendolyn Brooks

Don Lee wants

Don Lee wants
not a various America.
Don Lee wants
a new nation
under nothing;
a physical light that waxes; he does not want to
be exorcised, adjoining and revered;
he does not like a local garniture
nor any impish onus in the vogue;
is not candlelit
but stands out in the auspices of fire
and rock and jungle-flail;
wants
new art and anthem; will
want a new music screaming in the sun.

Gwendolyn Brooks

from **In the Mecca** *(1968)*
My name was changed to Haki Madhubuti in 1974.

The Good Man

For Haki.

In the time of detachment,

in the time of cold.

The good man.

He is still enhancer, renouncer.

In the time of detachment,

in the time of the vivid heather and affectionate evil,

in the time of oral

grave grave legalities of hate – all real

walks our prime registered reproach and seal.

Our successful moral.

The good man.

Watches our bogus roses, our rank wreath, our

love's unreliable cement, the gray

jubilees of our demondom.

Coherent

Counsel! Good man.

Require of us our terribly excluded blue.

Constrain, repair a ripped, revolted land.

Put hand in hand land over.

Reprove

the abler droughts and manias of the day
and a felicity entreat.

Love.
Complete
your pledges, reinforce your aides, renew
stance, testament.

Force our poor sense into your logics, lend
superlatives and prudence: to extend
our judgment-through the terse and diesel day;
to
singe, smite, beguile our own bewilderments away.
Teach barterers the money of your star.
In the time of detachment, in the time of cold, in this time
tutor our difficult sunlight.
Rouse our rhyme.

Gwendolyn Brooks

Gwendolyn Brooks and Haki R. Madhubuti at the Third World Press 20th Anniversary Celebration, circa 1987

Courtesy of Poet Eugene B. Redmond
Gwendolyn Brooks Young Poet Laureate Awards (L-R) Sterling Plumpp, Haki R. Madhubuti, Walter Bradford and Ranson Boykin

Haki R. Madhubuti and Gwendolyn Brooks, circa 1978

Haki R. Madhubuti and Gwendolyn Brooks, 1989

Acknowledgements

I would like to extend a special thanks and much gratitude to Rose Perkins, Quraysh Ali Lansana, Gwendolyn Mitchell, Tacuma Roeback and Denise Borel Billups.

Some of the poems in this collection have been previously published.

Gwendolyn Brooks: "Young Heroes–II: To Don at Salaam," the excerpt from "In the Mecca" and "The Good Man" published in *Blacks* (Third World Press, 1987). Reprint permission granted by Brooks Permissions, P.O. Box 19355 Chicago, IL 60619. For more information, please contact gbpermissions@aol.com.